BRANCHES

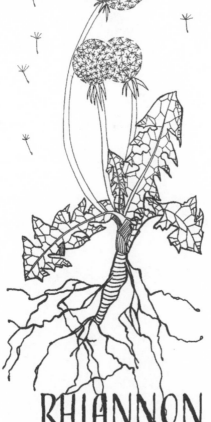

RHIANNON
MCGAVIN

McGavin, Rhiannon

ISBN: 978-1-945649-37-0

Edited by Safia Elhillo
Cover design by Cassidy Trier
Editorial design by Ian DeLucca

Not a Cult
Los Angeles, CA

Contents

Coda

Ignore the smog. You see what you want to
here. You have to peel the sky like a loquat. Focus on how
from high enough, it all gleams; a surge
of street lamps and restaurant neon, undercut
by steel bones whistling hot wind.
Los Angeles is all the waves at once.
It seems a fair trade for drowning out the stars. I know
there's a wall near my house
that has painted over slurs so often, the brick looks flesh.
The sun ripens as many bullets as tomatoes; the helicopters
fly lower. We didn't intend to stay. We planted perennials
and kept growing with that dip
in our front steps like an inhale, like a cupped hand,
it's where the rain pools when we get it,
when such blessings come in beams.
Not to brag but someone's scrawling ballads on the thick
of the red line because it's really too good to keep to themselves,
and I have been kissed in every theater downtown.
You know we had to tone down the concert hall?
Honey honey do I not hum the Metro melody? You are worth
the two buses and train it takes to get anywhere.
I'm scared I don't know enough to miss you
when I leave but I found dried jasmine in my suitcase
and my Fairfax penny shoes are so filled with sand,
I couldn't outrun you if I tried. Now lights up
on silent movies, and the ghosts of trolley cars
and when the San Andreas fault line gasps for fresh air,
when the seas rise, stick their chin out, and ask the entire coast
for the last dance at prom, and we all drown on the 110,
I will still be here, in old lion enclosures soaked in Shakespeare,
waiting for the stars to come back.

Girls

street-worth of neon just before west Hollywood,
splayed two-dimension with baby skin and
maraschino cherries   which   our bus drove past
180 mornings a year, as the fastest way to school
where we laugh at Sex: in the dictionary n draw
GIRLSGIRLSGIRLS
that are all circles too, rather than elbows and tissue like us
pants and skirt at the same time us
at home, teeter in our older sisters' high heels, the kind
she has to walk   2 blocks away before wearing, hickeyed
with sidewalk, hickeyed with chalk   we
saw the signs more than anything else
n do not know   what the names mean yet
except that none of us can bend like that   yet
we chew gum n make sure the boys see we can swallow it   it
will stay with us longer   we found a balloon in the soccer field
    damp as a milk carton

en rose

my mother says   bloom where you are planted
she would tuck me in with borrowed maps whispering
we were here and here
in boats and bakeries
she did not tell me we are also in the soil and air
i've never seen my mother's france
of cobblestones and blessed memory
or the town she thinks was ours
before the first train marched for drancy
she has to show me postcards instead of family pictures
she swears my bones are strong as rock
and i know every step i take is in mourning
to be jewish is to be born during a funeral
the graves hold no flowers
they are for the living   they don't grow fast enough
but there will always be more stones to stack in the cemetery
by a school   a bleeding kosher market
i am tired of counting
of these infinitives
everything sounds beautiful in french
the slurs echo like a crystal toast
maman i want to bloom like a summer rose
ima save me from the cuts of toulouse and marseilles
and paris and paris and paris
on est d'ici in our friday dinners and perfume
and the stained glass windows of the grand synagogue
in so many more colors than red
the white roses in our front yard wring pink from the soil
when i was younger i would lick rain off the flowers and think
this is what love tastes like
the blood when you bite your tongue singing
a lullaby so soft
the bullets can't find you

Ballet for Scoliosis

the school nurse found the hostage letter   stuck under my
right shoulder blade when I was 12   but I already knew
my joints cracked like fireworks   it was my fault for
slouching
   I still make the slow bend down   in these child shoes

 I grew sideways   all my big kid teeth came in
at the top of my spine   an s a hush   when I am
loud   when I move
  too fast   it grinds the match heads to spark

at the clinic   I recite symptoms in 5th position
   leotard loose as a johnny gown   but I'm only
moving deeper towards you   you who follows as posture
symmetry won't save me   so I grip the bar in the
community center   stretch around your torso   unspool
the lumbar nerves
I am in the beginner's studio I am a mile behind the music
    tell me
what to do   to unwind this spiral staircase   this swan beak

once a month I wake on a Sunday morning crying for too much
        or never
the mattress divots like boned fish as I get up

sore legs with nothing to show for it   the sweat
smells different here   a light glints from waxed wood
        my hair up
to keep it out of my face   out of you   off the floor
        you are supposed
I think to ask me if it hurts   you don't look at me
outside here   you spin me   onto my stomach   I close
my eyes and think of all the little ballerinas
under the sculptor's hand

the world rattles on the layer   between my organs and air
when I take my shirt off   the telegram crumples   chin up
neck long
here's another thing the girls in class can do   that I cannot
there are so many
   ways to check if I am pretty yet   I wear loud lipstick   so I
can see myself in the mirror   and nod

in the branches

all the ficus does is spit
berries that crumble to dry marrow   leaves the color of flu
ficus seethes beneath the surface
roots jut the sidewalk out like bone
don't ask me how it got there,

all I do is sweep
what it hacks up—
nightgowns   bandages   fistfuls of hair
and whole spirals of orange peels,
from someplace else, no wishes here
just ficus-filtered light
mottled and shaking in the branches
as the branches shake

where all I dream about
is chainsaws and forklifts.
I am collecting tools for the slaughter—
thick gloves, plastic goggles. I'll learn
to unravel without breaking, as tangerines do

Things that could Happen to a Girl wearing Jeans

Ari wears her jeans with the cuffs rolled up
like in a French film at the midnight cinema,
where we sneak malt milkshakes.

She's in a punk band, and all the holes
in her clothes are girl-made.
I wear my jean jacket to her shows, with pins older than me,
from my mother's days of denim.
I like the way fabric bears history,
with ultramarine cresting to frayed white. We are still
paint chips and copper chloride in every kind of blue;
charms watching us from the door frame,
echoed by the blue eyeshadow I streak to feel brave,
forget-me-nots on my street corner at dawn,
our mouths stained blue raspberry.

Julie writes notes on her pants so she doesn't forget
the exact shade of dawn from her rooftop, day after it rains
this way, when she's alone on the subway
she can look at her legs and feel genesis, while
flour and powdered sugar cover Nina's jean skirt, skipping
past her apron. Once me and Eva waited three hours
at Nina's apartment for her to come back
and make us grilled cheese. Eva walks with square shoulders,
one hand in her pocket, holding a guitar pick like an amulet

We are all each other's patches
and there is nothing so good
as your hair brushed and braided
by someone who loves you

I like my body best when I am dancing with my best friends
and someone spills their drink on me
and whipped cream joins the nail polish,
hot sauce, candle wax, those darling smears
we accumulate from living
I carry my heart like a pincushion
I know if I dance like this
these will not be the pants that I wore
when all my good words were not enough
when the decades choked
my hands cold as supreme court marble, no
                     no
these are the jeans that I hiked ten miles in,
just to pick wildflowers.

Art Class

In my kindergarten art class, sun dripped
through finger-paint-covered windows.
I learned the primaries: red blue yellow;
you could make the whole rainbow from three colors.
I'm older when I tell myself you only look
at the anatomy figure for reference, but this girl
made me understand why they say *pretty as a painting*.
You can't touch museum art. We have the same lotion,
it smells better on her.

I can't draw a straight line anymore, but that's alright,
her hair is naturally curly. A boy called her weird yesterday
and I wanted to tell her that I practice shading for hours
 to recreate the light in her eyes,
but it'd be clear I was staring;
you're not supposed to look at your friends like that.

Teacher says Prussian blue was created
when a chemist tried to birth a perfect red.
He added animal blood to the flask, and out burst
blue when ultramarine weighed more than gold.
I wanted vermilion like Romeo,
ruby as sunset flash, lipstick maroon forget-me-not kisses
I would take azure like sky on ocean,
school skirt navy hiding our hands
or even yellow sunflower petals, thick oil whispering
she loves you, she loves you, she loves you.

I swallow each pigment and wait for the antidote, I can't breathe
without coming into poison, it's apple seeds and seeping
through junior high gym floorboards when you watch
your best friend dance with boys who aren't you.

Girls carve through my diaries
like a pickpocket sketching the Hope diamond
I've lined my coat with looking
I've read the books, the poetry is good but
the author's picture on the back flap is black and white,
never watercolor, never wedding album.
I want to be five years old again, mixing all the colors
until I get the dark brown of her shoulder freckles,
and you give a valentine to everyone in class.

Freshet

I didn't know
lips could look that much like fruit slices
and here your smile has the circumference of a
tangerine. Now, you say good morning,
your back speckled as a spring egg.
I keep your name halfway
between maple syrup and honey, with a rush
of fresh water for the ocean. My washed hair
is perfume enough. You kiss my forehead.
Salmon belly, isn't it good to melt?

sonnet seventy-eight

Enough tea in your kitchen to spice a river,
all the boxes fall into each other on
one shelf, mint and ginger and something green with jasmine,
labels peel off into lilies
and dust simpering through dawn.
I take someone else's shirt and wipe
the counter clean. The kettle boils for
two cups, just two cups.

A church of rings on your wood table
(where you tried to teach me what
you thought the play was about) yet
here I am this morning with tender legs,
the place like warm ceramic, where your head rested
as I tripped over sonnets. Maybe
the water cycle doesn't apply
to me. The steam gets to stay on the shower wall.

The story where you spun me first on the blue tile won't change;
you are the most spring and me, your best-loved feather.

Pan Pacific Pool

every other day we hunt the library
for new installments of fantasy
dystopia comic thriller romance
and not a single late fee
we pick books best read by the pool next door
in this lucky park
where you play softball and i shout your name
we also have a pool
that drips off us in diamonds
while we trace tan lines from too-big swimsuits
one hour of your mother's work
exchanged for a whole summer day
a dollar for Youth Admission, four more
buy a hot dog (with onions) red soda
and chips please
we swear to try every ice cream flavor by September
and the bins of pastel become our calendar
when the lifeguards go on break
we eat on the grass in front
a chain in the flag pole clinks like drugstore change
ants on gingko branches swap secrets

Do you remember when
my hair was lime-green from chlorine
and the coolest you'd ever be
was shivering in the young adult section?
With a book, a damp towel, a stomach
like an upside-down cereal bowl.
We counted coins and pages and ate
until we were full. Would you believe
that I can stand in the deep end
but I still hold my breath?

Garlic breath

Damn the fire alarm. My pasta is
fine. Serrated knife to slice tomatoes,
leftover water for thick sauce, and since
the ventilation is one clogged window,
you fan smoke away with a baking pan.
It's an easy meal, and we have been
simple with each other across kitchens.
While you rinse freckles of dirt from button
mushrooms, I set my heart on the table.
I'm so used to chasing after my breath,
it occurs to me as I chop basil,
we could argue as well with my head on your chest.

If I kiss you now it would taste like garlic
we would both taste like garlic

the creeps

yesterday we went hiking and i told you how
my mother's best friend was murdered
when they were a few years older than us
her ex choked her and the jury
wasn't allowed to know
he had a history of abuse

when the late august flies tried
to lick the sweat from my face
you blew them away with quick breaths
one hand on my jaw to keep me still

but it's why i'm afraid of men
and the wood grown to protect them
because yesterday
i wanted to believe the trees near your house
have never clapped with a gavel
but under your nails
you let the dirt of your fathers rot

Chanel No. 1941

Little black cloud unrolled over the camp.
A pile of wedding rings melted for the logo.
Even baby teeth look like pearls from a distance.

Wet lip dazzles cracks to rust
but no one does red like Coco.

What smoke bears your sky?
Are you clean if the soap is made from a body?

Sweet almond silage the bottle reads
Apply the zyklon to pulse points and rub.

Mom pats latkes from one hand to the other
scent on her wrists and neck humming.

the lab

how easy it was to test
the body's freezing temperature
with nothing but German snow for miles
scientifically   kilometers

a silver glint   is it
a scalpel   or a knife

Pain Theory
"You can't read the rat's mind. He won't talk to you and you can't read their minds. So you can never, ever, as a matter of principle, you can never, ever, be sure."   Gary Bennett, 1999

Once upon a time

Descartes took an ax to a tree and
struck the trunk in one spot, the
shock traveling

to the utmost leaf and back again, and
the tree said Ouch and Descartes noted it
and it was good

Buchner tied his loose tooth to the
radiator and ran backwards to wrench
out a cranial tube, kept rubbing the
gum with his poet's tongue. Melzack and Wall

explain knock knock jokes

to the dorsal horn. Cajal's neurons

dive into silver waves.

Before the flood

my handwriting was much neater. I
categorized my chicken pox scabs by
shape and location.

I haven't broken a bone. I don't recall
how spraining my fingers sounded,
although it happened enough. You
could ask what I was doing, hitting a
tetherball so hard that my hands
swelled, but I'll

talk of lightning.

These beautiful problems that
slip through my blood,

I could pretend I never felt anything
deeper than the blackberry ravine,

Most of the theory was discovered
by accident

The hospital poster reads
On a scale from one to ten
how accurately
can you predict rain?
When do
you start waiting for the needle to hit skin?
Studies have shown that
injuries orbit each other.
Pain the pocketwatch, the time traveler,
a vital sign, a compass,
whatever and wherever
some thousand natural blisters and burns:
proof the vagus nerve is
a willow thrumming
gently but quick
with wind chimes at the stomach, lungs
and heart
all bold echo.

mapping all the red pricks
in the mirror
looking for the punchline

I bandage my bare skin
and wait for someone
to ask what happened.

It hurts for everyone the first time
I don't remember how
the first time hurt.
They said the storm was in my head.
You heal and it's a chance to go home
or is it the other way around?
You wince like your grandparents and
my best blessing is
that nothing removes my own blood
as well as my own spit. Before I laugh it off
it must be felt and that
will never, ever, weigh more than
my witness.
I say this
to keep your eyes clear
trained on mine
unwavering
while I pull out the thorn.

Poll worker

I say Have a sticker! over laughter
from the owner of the real estate office
where the polling place was housed.
He starts giggling around sunset
as time zones hit the map on TV
over and over and the blood
known to be in the soil
splashes his loafers. I count the ballots
in stacks of ten. I count to a thousand
twice to check. This democracy
with a full electoral college
and empty voter registrations
relies on the peaceful transfer of power
such as a collection plate or a baseball bat.
They announce the election results
on the anniversary of Kristallnacht.
Glass breaks any way you cut it
and this is how mid-Manhattan
looks like Berlin. The man grabs the
podium
with both hands.
All summer I saw the signs
loaded on lawns and now
the bullet holes singe my lap.
If I had a girl
I'd marry her in a patchwork dress
and before I tear my journals to scraps
and feed the paper to a half-empty bottle
and light the match
and throw it as far as tired can throw
I will memorize the love poems
so I can recite them to her
in whatever dawn we have.

Chick Lit

Edgar Allen Poe said
The death of a beautiful woman is unquestionably
the most poetical topic in the world   except I think
the most poetic thing is the dress my mom wore
in France when she was pregnant. Yellowed with flowers,
stretched to fit her and shrinks to hold me now.
There's a sonnet in each of my nana's old lipsticks,
and all the coats my aunt wears,
another device in any piece of clothing deemed lucky.
In fact, the poetry is my neighbor
explaining how her parents survived a genocide
that spoke four languages, or maybe
the enjambment sobs in the shower, fruit aisle,
and best friend's car sinking through deep summer.
All our injuries rhyme, from singing with a sore throat
to a mattress heavier than God,
the freckle on my right palm, tracing every capillary popped
on purpose and stomach caesuras, who else
could place scars into genres?
I've seen better poems in rising bread
than anything Bukowski dreamed of,
that Hemingway demanded, and Sartre petitioned for.
They can excuse scaring women for art
though if you are a scared woman,
they tie your art back to your crazy,
like it's crazy how a couple movies
are worth more than children, like
they can't see the fingerprints on the film strip
and I guess it's a good song but that bass drum
sounds like internal bruising and I can't dance at all.

The violence of creative men is more
of a burning library than a closed book
but choose what you want to read   thus I concur,
that picking graveyard dirt out of my nails
is of highest literary value,
thus, the most poetical topic is me,
slumped on my desk, sleeping through every English class
for the rest of the year after my teacher said
he didn't know of any female writers good enough to study.
No one, in that damned mob of scribbling women,
was worth discussion
since we were only supposed to be
the flourish / adverb / stage he walks on / spit on his finger
 so he can flip a page
and we can't bite the hand that feeds us, can't
swat away pens that dip in our pretty corpses.
He sweats corn syrup and   red dye and
needs someone to hurt for him
yet I can stand straight without balancing his blood on my head.
I have always washed my troubles in extra mascara
so they are defined in the spotlight, molded them to hold
a rapier for the finale, taught them how to speak
from the gut even when crying, to project
so all the women who ever pressed
their thumb onto my cheek can watch me live from the back row
and the ghosts above the theater, they can see us too.

I could eat mulberry leaves

to soften my eyes the way you want

In the planetarium, you smirk at Earth, blue speck
barely there, pinned against a swarming galaxy
I'm a smithereen too
flush with life even if nobody notices
I've seen every angle of the night
from your glares and bored nods I could pull a constellation
a romance to be guided by
but you'll never hold me to the light
I won't floss with your name
so I have no lover
I just watch the sun rise

me and the silk worms go home

Doomsday Vault

Freedom is not someone else choosing how you die
and this isn't the first time you've thought about it,
since it's in the news,

but you wanted to see the killer's face as it happened

instead of strangers in secure rooms
people who prepared fear into legal tender
and made the world into a bad poem,
who forgot that gold can't spackle a fallout shelter
but wanted their meals fast anyway.

You took three-minute showers and ate no meat
and everything happened.
You cut your hair and swallowed your credit cards
and nothing changed.

In Norway, a hundred thousand seeds clutch the legs
of a school desk in an unstaffed facility.

The sidewalks of your neighborhood
peel from the earth like rotting wallpaper
The windows of office buildings plucked out as fingernails
The cemetery bronze with pennies

You decide that the sun is one greasy coin
placed squarely over your eyes
You walk the edge of a glacier
with a hand covering the exposed skin of your neck.

Potatoes sleep beneath metal, snug with a vow of harvest.

early September

I leave in my summer dress
because I'm afraid of a new year with its locked air of luggage
a cold I may not feel when all I wanted was feeling
I wanted a blue jacket that smelled like thyme and you

told me   it had been the sweetest sleep
The museums could be shuddered and swept off.
We had orange juice and warm bread, discussed tyrants
between bites of raspberry on a bench at the station.
A kiss goodbye, you ask me to stay safe
& I bet you say that
to all the American girls.

A bullet on the horizon, we saw
the train advance
& wave a flag of ash
& a suitcase stranded on the tracks below us.
I wasn't surprised when the train crushed it under a mob
of wheels
but I still winced at the fracture of metal
as the clothes swirled from the husk like ghosts.

I knew the most hidden corner of your neighborhood
& I know what drawer keeps my passport
& I watch the smoke drift far.

Making great art

Now more than ever, yes, specifically, us, at this darling
political moment, this heartening social juncture, that
unveils its saturated horrors as a rose, no, a narcissus, no,
a lobster claw pares away to present to us, with our bin-
ocular insight, with antiseptic and butter, our sacred duty,
which we have prepared for, though the civic situation is
worse than anything we, certainly, could have imagined,
our salient role in exhuming whatever lies profound at the
crossroads, such a weighted homage, such a doting honor
to live, yes, us, living, during this deeply interesting era,
to birth the movements we will be remembered for, that
which will bear clarity, as the sun, no, a magnifying glass,
no, a stream of ants, although we do wish there was more
quiet to write by, although the work, the all-consumed
travail, practically writes itself now, more than ever, now,
how wise are we to lean off the shore of danger with black
milk lapping at our clever heels so that finally, all that we
struggled against has been made corporeal and we can
shake its wet hand for the position, finally the head rolls
across our platform to spit the greatest poem of all time in
a froth

Next year, in Paris

I see the city like a film every time I blink,
and this is how I know that I am wicked, but there's
always laundry. I can enunciate through a bar of soap,
say hello and thank you, blink away plastic wrap and terror

except it won't matter.
Next year, every machine of war becomes a greenhouse.
Inch plant sprawls through the halls of law
same as back home.
I bicycle along a river where night laps only water
with the safety to be lost and foolish anyplace.

Streets braided around my wrist,
I fold prayers into any wall, carry charms back to my mother
in this state of a knapsack, from the open shutters of my chest
I fly the last visas and that birthright of
a clean dress and wet hair is mine too.

POST-WINTER

TREE:

   Murdermouth carried me here   I cracked
through lockjaw here in this forest of precious stone
 where I am the only thing un-petrified   that could look
like home   I was never tall enough to climb
 they pick my rind like their own skins   I understand
I have also mistaken pyre for sunlight   let the spring-ache
trick me   been too lush for my own good
my leaves flash green   as coins at the bottom of a well
   look how much i carry   my fruit   my atriums
puckered   a stone to swallow   He says   she bit first
men have the alphabet   and allot these stories
if all the sisters and nieces and cousins
laughed in a forest   could that be a legend?   Let me hear
a myth where you survive   honey   I am sorry
    for whoever saw you asleep on the couch
and left the party   who watched you at the gas station
with a man and kept driving
   I'm sorry for how sound my roots go
You   another red blot in my rings
polish me to a hilt   I don't want to be a coffin anymore
see sometimes   I'm the only food
in the graveyard   but if they write on me   I say
how the story ends

HADES:

You get lonely when you're immortal. She
charmed me with that hummingbird heartbeat, made
me kiss her eyes close on a night long as
heaven. That's all I care about, doe eyes
and an easy smile. I'm a sucker
for dimples, with a veil of blush drawn close
around her, I mean, what else could you do
but love? Listen, it's not my fault you have
to smile to say my name right. You want
the fruit when it's mellow and sweet and not
a day later. It's natural, it's a
given. All I am is a trellis. I
took nothing.

PERSEPHONE:

well   i threw up all the seeds in the motel
bathroom then took my pulse with the same fingers
pulled on that little dress and i guess the dogs
were asleep. i cut

my teeth on a bike chain. i double-knotted
my sneakers and pedaled with sore legs, bad sore,
not like when i swam the whole day. anyway
think it was around

five since since the stars were fading out and there were
old women knitting, you know, waiting for the
train. i smiled at them. i'm grown up now too.
what i remember

most of his kiss, his whole mouth evergreen mint
like he had to be clean on purpose. i don't
know how many times he died over me. he
told me fruit spoiled

if you waited too long and i am so smart
for my age. he had rugged stubble and eyes
for hanging. i could never tell what side of
the rope he was on,

he kissed my neck like a scythe and it's not my
fault i kissed back, i was little, i am still
picking it from my lip, he popped amber on
my skin, traced coils

around my ankles, made me think it was his
love in my good heart, not the deadbolt, that kept
us close. his room a body that bid me stay,
his body a room

locked. i bet he bragged to the dust, told them how
i cried, tugged hard at his sleeve. weren't you sixteen
and sick for it once? a match is struck behind
your eyes and you must

smother it before anyone takes notice,
takes you. i felt tall. i felt taller than a
sheath. he promises to soothe the buzz and thresh
of femoral and

carotid. our ashes mixed red in the
honeyed nest then doused with wine. and then morning.
under the mattress, the concrete blocks were the
same shade as any

grave. i hold a bus token to the center
of my forehead. it doesn't matter how i
was razed, only that he was there to catch me.
that he could be a

ditch and gravity. his chest fit to collapse
upon. it's power, i thought. buried in a
man with the little deaths he rendered from me.
i asked what he saw

afterwards when he closed his eyes. fields, he said
fields rolling and endless and my love the lone
lantern. my name molded to the shape of his
mouth. he tied a ring

of clover to fit my finger and i was
so happy to be a woman. when i left
home, i wore the perfume he gave me. i would
spray the air above

and before me and dance through that fog. those blue
atoms of pearl smelled like sweat by the third week.
for my first shower alone after six months
i clogged every cleft

in the bathroom with towels until i could
walk on steam. they give me soft clothes, comb the bees
from my hair and label them in bags.
i identify

him: host of many screams. my villain. the un-
husband. he'd exhausted himself that night. i
knew how to trim the heads off dry daisies so
new blossoms can live,

to prune rose stems at a slant, to blow the teeth
from a dandelion. he had wind in him
when i left, i ran until my whole body
was freshet, i crossed

rivers of traffic and daffodils sprang from
roadkill, poppies bloomed from the bicycle seat,
i laid my lipsticks on the subway tracks, watched
the seven o'clock

crush his sex. when i came up from underground
i knew how to get home. i ran to feel the
orange tile of the kitchen i grew up
in warm on my bare

feet. i chose to be a girl who doesn't want
to die. the birds ask O PERSEPHONE HOW
i say i don't care about kings and shepherds,
no deity can outlast

the only child of a single mother.

no god's stronger than me.

Parameters

I've decided that you get to choose what
counts as a first kiss. Some parameters:
You're awake. You want to. The person cares

about you, and you think they're swell, for a
full moment. Only on your knees if you're
both crouching. And none of it hurts, free of

dares and bleach. There is no submission
to power because their teeth are as sharp
as yours. You have a heartbeat. Pick your kiss

like lilac flush in June, and it is real.
Maybe no fireworks? Maybe nothing
burns past the skin for once. Crumple up the

harm. It won't matter. I've thrown away six
first kisses so far. Banish by any
ceremony you please. Drop it down a

canyon. Laugh it off like a snob. With this
fish bone, coax the corsage out from under
your bed. Catch it in a jar, grind the glass

under your heel. Soak it in salt water
until it's breath again. You can wade out
up to your hips, looking for something worth

keeping. Good kisses shine even out of
the sea. There are keys and velvet shoes, know
this, a world of bridges beyond your long

walk home. I pin my hair with a favorite
kiss, I stir another into coffee,
and all day the dandelion seeds of

good kisses whistle through the sky
and bloom wherever you wish

First Base Gold

My Song of Songs is stained: beach salt up the spine,
highlighter waltzing through divine verse,
thumbprints of powdered sugar from last week's doughnuts.
The book yawns on the grass now, green scratches
to a violin beat, while you're talking to the prophets
because you   at the back of the Hebrew classroom
you swore that there was more scripture in my braids.
Your hair flakes into remnants of fire. We are constructing
the Ringstrasse on American passports
and Gustav trails his brush from rooftop to cobblestone.
I heard he painted his subjects totally naked before adding clothes
(my great-aunt's necklace got caught in your collar)
and the kids dance in museums while
howling city elders make Philosophy, Medicine,
and Jurisprudence put gym shirts on and go home early yet
Gustav was the sort of man who had whipped cream for breakfast,
sweet tooth sharp, breaking mosaics like bread with his neighbors,
they knocked down the boundary walls to build second society
in sacred spring and Klimt is swirling eight types
of gold leaf in his Manischewitz shot.
I am looking carefully at his jour dames,
their crooked fingers and noses
and how thick hair captures candles so glorious
can't he frame my mirror too?
(I think I hear my cousin calling)
Those girls, celestial, wound to us, improbable,
they must have walked boulevards
alongside men who returned sketches to ash, with too much poison
for charcoal to draw out

the Judiths, Salomes, and Shulamites, covered in caves,
baptized, heads shaved, Mendel's fists locked around
his camera on the death march
perhaps the greatest design was the need for documentation
to keep pencils in throat   to drag nails through cement
but nazis stay dead and

Henryk and Stefania are digging up what they buried in Lodz:
the negatives hidden in his coat as she watched for guards
their wedding echoes through crushed windows
all my love for a slingshot
on the projector slide, I see evidence of honeycomb preserved
(my) arm around (your) neck, blurry with a slow shutter
there's never been a better place to kiss than circled by lilies,
sunflowers swallowing lead and
we, at the back of the Hebrew classroom
we do not know their names but your eyelashes are so long
that they touch my cheeks when we are close enough
and I have never heard the mourner's
my degenerate, shall we rend our clothes for joy?
What a blessing, to see myself in brownest of brown eyes,
better than wine

here we stand, three hours to a full moon
here we lie, at the bottom of the century
I mean on top I mean
picture to picture, kiss to kiss
you and me in the synagogue garden,
full square, soaked in first base gold.

Golem Song

I am flour on the cutting board
I'm mud from the river bottom I'm chalk clapped out
I'm ink in a thumbprint and paper pulp bleached for the page
I'm pebbles chiseled from tablets to make letters in relief
I'm cookie crumbs on the alphabet
I'm resin flakes on a smuggled violin
gold soot of a jeweler's kit   I'm a pile of rings
I'm a powdered nose I'm spit in the exhale
I'm lint of a sweater you forgot to wear before leaving the house
I'm stitches in a hemline
I'm dandruff   I'm mothballs in a wedding dress
and the dust kicked up from dancing
in the organ pipes   an almond blossom
When a pomegranate breaks then
I'm the seed in a split lip
I'm brine around scrolls and vegetables, I'm sugar
on a doughnut, I'm what you want most
on a Saturday morning I'm yeast & hot water
I'm medication stirred into yogurt
I'm atoms rocking back & forth in place
I'm the last morsel   I'm the first stone
I am a bullet if I need to be
I'm all the rocks in your graveyard
I'm motes floating in light that did get through the cracks

I am earth unmended
Anyone made to swallow this dirt   Any unmarked field
is your family   I am ash & I am ash
& you will not ever forget this name

Foreign Correspondent

though there are churches along the paper route
it is my pleasure to report
that I have been picked up and spun in front of the cathedral
a few steps off the island and missed curfew
all the notebooks rang out
on assignment for the empire of memory
I was lovely comma lovely for nearly seven hours
I read verses and none of them were mine

Prayer for the new year

For the new year, I won't count it down like a
uranium bomb. The last days
came as a plague ship over the horizon, I
know, so I'm swimming to meet it. Let the
desert bloom through ruins we can look out of, let us
outlive the wolves. Fresh air is the only kiss I
need and I will carry you like honey and
apples. Bless the body between
love and fear, bless who
dares the skyline, and who holds
thieves accountable from lamp posts as
red dandelions blaze and what's the future except an
unfolded table cloth?
Midnight led by the shifting light of wounds across white rose
petals? I
           I will
            I will see
                I will see the moon and morning and hope.

Acknowlegements

So many people and places have fostered my writing over the years.

I want to thank my family and league of godparents for supporting my strange habits. Not A Cult truly made this book possible, and Branches wouldn't exist without the incredible work of Ian, Daniel, and Hollis.

Thank you first readers and always friends: Ariela, Sam, Eden, Mehtab, Arabelle, and Max.

Thank you Daniel Schaefer for being a poet with a camera.

I have so much gratitude towards the wonderful teachers at the Los Angeles Drama Club, Get Lit, Urban Word, and YoungArts for fostering creative spaces for young people, as well as the kind folks who helped me work the copy machines at Staples as I made my teen zines, and my elementary school librarian Carole Koneff, and my slam coaches Alyesha Wise and Matthew Cuban for making sure I knew to leave it on the stage.

I would also like to thank my English teachers, especially the bad ones.

About the Author

Rhiannon McGavin has failed the CA driver's license test times so far. She has performed from the Hollywood Bowl to the Library of Congress, as well as on NPR. Her work has been published by Tia Chucha Press, Teen Vogue, and Button Poetry. As a YoungArts Finalist in Spoken Word, she was nominated for the Presidential Scholar of the Arts. Rhiannon was the Youth Poet Laureate of Los Angeles in 2016, and currently studies literature at UCLA.

9 781945 649370